Sally J. Castillo

Freeze Candy Delights

(Vol 2) - A New Chapter of Innovative Freeze-Dried Candy Recipes for Sweet Creations!

Disclaimer

Contents

Note: All recipe in this cookbook yields five servings
feel free to adjust to your preference.

Introduction

"You are welcome back to the fanciful world of freeze-dried candy making!" Vol 2 of the 'Freeze Candy Delights' series will take you on another mouth-watering experience. We're excited to bring you a new batch of enticing recipes and inventive approaches to help you improve your candy-making talents. Prepare to be amazed once again as we discover new tastes, intriguing textures, and fascinating inventions that will leave you wanting more. This book is your passport to a world of sweet pleasures, whether you're a seasoned candy aficionado or a passionate newbie. So come along with us as we reveal a new chapter in the art of freeze-dried candy manufacturing!"

Candies that have been subjected to the freeze-drying technique are collectively known as "freeze-dried candy." The moisture is removed from the candy as it is frozen, creating a treat that is light, and crisp, and can be stored for a long time without going bad. This method of preservation extends the candy's shelf life without compromising its taste, texture, or appearance.

The candy is first frozen, then transferred to a vacuum chamber where the moisture is sublimated or changed straight from solid ice to vapor without going through the liquid stage. This process evaporates the bulk of the water, leaving behind a dry confection.

Freeze-dried sweets are known for their unique crunch, which is light and airy. Fruit snacks, candy, chocolate-covered goodies, and even novelty shapes are all fair game. Common types of freeze-dried sweets include fruit-flavored chocolate-coated fruit snacks, fruit-flavored fruit chips, and fruit-flavored rings.

Freeze-dried candy has a longer storage life than regular candy. Freeze-dried sweets have a low moisture content, making them suitable for long-term storage without spoiling. Because of this, they are often used as a lightweight snack when traveling or while out in the wilderness.

In the kitchen, freeze-dried sweets are used for a variety of purposes, including but not limited to garnishing desserts, adding flavor to baked products, and topping ice cream and yogurt. Their concentrated taste and distinct consistency make them a welcome addition to many dishes.

The following are some guidelines for effective freeze drying:

Properly prepare the items: Preparing the materials correctly is essential before freeze-drying them for long-term storage. Suitable preparation may include washing, slicing, or arranging them. Freeze-drying will occur more consistently in equally sized parts.

Pre-freeze the items: It is typically advised that the products be pre-frozen before being placed in the freeze dryer for optimal results. This aids in keeping the structure together and avoiding clumping when it freezes.

Use a vacuum-sealed container: Put the objects in a vacuum-sealed bag or container before putting them in the

Freeze Candy Delights

freeze drier to keep out as much air and moisture as possible. This helps prevent oxidation and preserves the quality.

Optimal temperature and pressure settings: For best results, adjust your freeze dryer's temperature and pressure according to the manufacturer's recommendations. The model and the food being freeze-dried may need different adjustments.

Keep an eye on the drying time: Drying times might vary widely depending on the brand or the recipe you're using. Loss of quality may occur from either over- or under-drying, depending on the substance being dried.

Allow proper cooling after drying: After the freeze-drying process is finished, the products need time to cool down before the freeze-drier can be opened or they may be packaged. This aids in preventing the environment's moisture from being absorbed.

Store in suitable conditions: Freeze-dried goods should be kept in vacuum-sealed bags or other airtight containers in cold, dry, dark areas. This keeps them fresh for a longer period of time and helps them keep their quality.

Experiment with different items and recipes: Don't be afraid to try out new goods and recipes with freeze-drying since there are so many options available. Freeze-drying works well for many different types of food, including fruits, vegetables, meats, herbs, and even dairy products.

Keep a record of successful recipes: Make sure to keep track of your best freeze-drying recipes, including the drying time, temperature, and any tweaks you made along the way. This will allow you to repeat the procedure with similar outcomes in the future.

Practice patience: Freeze drying might take many hours or even days, so you'll need to be patient. Having patience is essential for achieving positive outcomes. If you care about the quality of the end result, you shouldn't hurry the process.

Keep in mind that the scope of this advice is broad. For the greatest results, you should always follow the manufacturer's guidelines for using your freeze dryer.

Traditional Formulas for Freeze-Dried Sweets

Dehydrated Strawberries for Snacking

15-minute prep time.
Hardness: Very Simple
Five servings

Ingredients
- 450 grams, or 1 pound, of fresh strawberries

Instructions
1. Strawberries should be washed in cold water for a few minutes. Use a kitchen paper to dab them.

2. Strawberry green tops should be removed and thrown away.

3. Thinly and uniformly slice the strawberries. Cut the meat into pieces between 1/8 and 1/4 inch thick.

4. Prepare your freeze drier by laying out the strawberry slices in a single layer on the trays.

5. Follow the freeze dryer's directions for drying strawberries after placing the trays inside. Adjust the thermostat and watch to the suggested settings.

6. Launch the freeze-drying process and wait for the strawberries to become dry and crisp. Depending on the kind of freeze dryer you have, this might take several hours or perhaps a whole night.

7. Remove the trays from the freeze-drier and set the strawberry chips aside to cool to room temperature after the freeze-drying process is complete.

8. Seal the resealable bags or transfer the airtight container with the freeze-dried strawberry chips to store them.

As a healthy and tasty snack, you may enjoy your own freeze-dried strawberry chips.

Freeze-drying time is not included in the preparation time since it varies widely across freeze-dryer models and settings.

Bananas cut and dried in the freezer

Ten-Minute Preparation Time
Hardness: Very Simple
Five servings

Ingredients
- Five perfectly ripe bananas

Instructions
1. Bananas should be peeled and cut into even, circular slices approximately a quarter of an inch thick.

2. Line a baking sheet with parchment paper or a silicone baking mat and spread the banana slices in a single layer. Ensure there is sufficient space between slice.

3. Banana slices should be frozen for at least two to three hours, or until they are solid and unmovable, on a baking sheet in the freezer.

4. When the banana slices have frozen solid, place them in the freeze drier. Spread the slices out in a single layer, with some room in between them for ventilation.

5. Set the freeze dryer's timer and temperature according to the manual. Freeze-drying bananas typically takes 24 to 48 hours at a temperature of 0 to -20 degrees Fahrenheit (-18 to -29 degrees Celsius).

6. Prepare the bananas for freeze-drying by subjecting them to primary and secondary drying until they are totally dry and crisp. The freeze dryer type and the thickness of the slices will determine the precise drying time.

7. Banana slices may be freeze-dried in a single layer and then removed from the trays to be stored in airtight containers or vacuum-sealed bags.

Banana slices that have been freeze-dried may be consumed or used as a tasty and nutritious topping for yogurt, desserts, and baked products, among other things. If you want to revive them, all it takes is a quick soak in water.

Keep in mind that if you want your freeze-dried banana slices to keep their crisp texture and taste, you should store them in a cold, dry spot that is out of the reach of moisture and sunlight.

If you're using a different freeze drier model or your banana slices are a different thickness, the drying time I've listed above may change. To get the most out of your freeze-dryer, make sure to read and follow all of the manufacturer's instructions.

Dehydrated Apple Slices

15-minute prep time.
Hardness: Very Simple

Ingredients
- Five apples, about the size of a medium.
- Extract one lemon
- A mixture of cinnamon sugar for dusting is optional.

Instructions
1. To remove any residue or debris, wash the apples under running water. Use a fresh towel to pat them dry.

2. Use an apple core or a knife to remove the cores from the apples. Take off the core and the seeds so that the apple is hollow.

3. Apples should be sliced into transverse rings approximately 14 inches (0.6 cm) thick. Apples with their peels on provide more fiber and nutrients than apples without their peels.

4. Toss the apple rings in the freshly squeezed lemon juice and set aside. Coat the rings evenly by lightly tossing them. The acid in the lemon juice keeps the food from becoming brown and gives it a nice flavor.

5. Make sure the apple rings aren't overlapping when you spread them out on the freeze-drying trays or racks. When freeze-drying, make sure there is adequate room for air to move in and out of the rings.

6. Follow the freeze dryer's manual for drying time and temperature after placing the trays inside. The time it takes depends on the freeze dryer you choose. Freeze-drying usually takes a few hours to finish.

7. After the apple rings have been freeze-dried, take them out of the freezer and let them cool to room temperature.

8. Sprinkle a cinnamon sugar mixture over the freeze-dried apple rings for more taste, if preferred. If you like the apples in their raw form, there's no need to do anything at all.

9. To keep the freeze-dried apple rings crisp and flavorful, store them in an airtight container or vacuum-sealed bags. They'll keep for months if left at room temperature.

You can eat these freeze-dried apple rings as a snack, mix them into yogurt or cereal, or use them in baked goods.

I really think this recipe will come in handy. Don't hesitate to ask additional questions if you have them.

Pineapple chunks, freeze-dried: a tasty recipe

Ten-Minute Preparation Time
Hardness: Very Simple

Ingredients
- Only 1 ripe pineapple

Instructions
1. Peel the pineapple and cut off the rough center before using it. Pineapple should be cut into bite-sized pieces. For even freeze drying, make sure they are of the same size.

2. Line a baking sheet or pan with parchment paper and spread the pineapple pieces out in a single layer. Make sure there is breathing room between the components.

3. Freeze the tray of pineapple pieces until they are absolutely solid. This ensures that the pineapple will retain its form and structure after being freeze-dried.

4. After the pineapple is frozen into pieces, move them to the freeze drier. Set the temperature and pressure levels recommended by the manufacturer for use with fruits.

5. Get the freeze dryer going, and let it do its thing according to the manual. Depending on the pineapple's moisture content and the freeze-dryer type, this may take anything from several hours to a whole day.

6. Wait for the freeze drier to cool down before removing the pineapple pieces from it. This aids in the reduction of environmental moisture absorption.

7. Carefully take the frozen pineapple chunks out of the freeze drier and store them in a vacuum-sealed bag or other airtight container. If you care about keeping their quality, you should get rid of as much air as you can.

8. Keep the freeze-dried pineapple chunks out of the light and in a cold, dry area. They retain their original taste and texture even after being preserved for a long time.

9. Use the freeze-dried pineapple chunks as a tasty topping for yogurt and cereal, or enjoy them on their own as a nutritious snack.

Note that freeze-dried pineapple chunks may be utilized in a variety of ways outside only snack foods like granola bars and tropical smoothies.

Blueberry Drops, Freeze Dried

Ten-Minute Preparation Time
Effort Required: Low

Ingredients
- Blueberries, enough for 2 cups
- Lemon juice, 1 tablespoon
- Optional: 1 tablespoon of honey

Instructions
1. Blueberries should be washed in cold water and patted dry with a paper towel.

2. Blueberries, lemon juice, and honey (if used) should be mixed together in a bowl. Carefully mix so that the blueberries are equally coated.

3. Spread the blueberries out evenly on the freeze dryer's trays. It's important to give the blueberries some room to breathe by leaving some distance between them.

4. Follow the freeze dryer's directions for fruit freeze-drying and load the trays inside.

5. Get your freeze dryer going, and let it 12 to 24 hours to dry whatever it is you're trying to preserve, depending on the model and how dry you want it.

6. Carefully take the blueberries from the trays after they have been freeze-dried and are crisp.

7. To keep the freeze-dried blueberries fresh, place them in an airtight container or resealable bags.

These freeze-dried blueberry drops are perfect as a quick and nutritious snack or as a sweet addition to your favorite cereal, yogurt, dessert, or baked product. Their crisp texture and bold blueberry taste make them a treat.

If you don't have access to a freeze drier, you may try using your home freezer to get the same effect, albeit the texture and outcomes may be different.

Raspberry Crunchies, Freeze-Dried

Ten-Minute Preparation Time
Effort Required: Low

Ingredients:
- Raspberries, enough for 2 cups
- Granulated sugar, 2 tablespoons

Instructions

1. The raspberries should be washed in cold water and dried gently on a paper towel.

2. Toss the raspberries with some granulated sugar in a large basin. Gently toss the raspberries to provide a uniform coating.

3. Spread the sugared raspberries out in a single layer on the freezer drying trays. Make sure there's enough room for air to circulate around the raspberries.

4. Place the trays into the freeze drier and adjust the settings so that the fruit will dry out.

5. Start up your freeze dryer and let it dry for the specified amount of time, usually anywhere from 12 to 24 hours.

6. When the raspberries have reached the desired crispness from freeze-drying, they should be removed from the pans and allowed to cool.

7. Keep the freeze-dried raspberry crunchies fresh for as long as possible by transferring them to an airtight container or resealable bags.

Raspberry crunchies that have been freeze-dried make for a tasty and sour standalone snack. You can sprinkle them over yogurt, cereal, or ice cream, or even bake with them to give your treats an extra crunch and flavor boost.

If you don't have access to a freeze drier, you may try using your home freezer to get the same effect, albeit the texture and outcomes may be different.

Mango Lollypops, Frozen in Time

15-minute prep time.
Level of Difficulty: Average

Ingredients
- (Two) ripe Mangoes
- Lemon juice, 1 tablespoon
- Granulated sugar, one tablespoon (optional).
- Five sticks of lollipop

Instructions
1. Mangoes need to be peeled and the flesh separated from the pit. Thinly and consistently slice the mango flesh.

2. Mango slices may be kept from turning brown if they are tossed with lemon juice in a basin. Mango slices may be made sweeter by tossing them in granulated sugar.

3. Insert a lollipop stick into the bottom middle of each mango slice gently.

4. Spread the mango slices out on the freeze dryer's trays, leaving some room between them.

5. Follow the freeze dryer's directions for fruit freeze-drying and load the trays inside.

6. Get your freeze dryer going, and let it 12 to 24 hours to dry whatever it is you're trying to preserve, depending on the model and how dry you want it.

7. Take the mango slices out of the trays after they have been freeze-dried and crispy.

8. Mango lollipops should be stored in an airtight container or individually wrapped in transparent cellophane bags, once the sticks have been carefully removed.

9. Sweet and tropical tastes come together perfectly in these freeze-dried mango lollipops. As a snack or for celebrations, they are a delightful and refreshing option.

If you don't have access to a freeze drier, you may try using your home freezer to get the same effect, albeit the texture and outcomes may be different.

These freeze-dried mango lollipops are a lot of fun to make and eat.

Pineapple Rings, Freeze-Dried

15-minute prep time.
Effort Required: Low

Ingredients
- 2 fully ripe pineapples
- Lemon juice, about 2 teaspoons
- Honey or sugar (up to two teaspoons) is optional.

Instructions
1. To prepare pineapples, peel them and cut off the core. Pineapples should be sliced into rings that are approximately 14 inches thick. To do this, you'll need either a pineapple corer or a sharp knife.

2. Mix the pineapple rings, lemon juice, and some sweetener (honey or sugar) in a bowl. Gently toss the rings to obtain a uniform coating.

3. Arrange the pineapple rings in a single layer on the freeze dryer's trays, being sure to allow some room between each one so air may circulate freely.

4. Put the trays in the freeze drier and adjust the settings for freeze-drying fruits as directed by the manufacturer.

5. Launch the freeze-drying procedure and let it complete its cycle for the specified amount of time (usually 12−24 hours, depending on your freeze-dryer type and desired dryness).

6. Carefully take the freeze-dried pineapple rings from the trays and set them aside to cool.

7. Keep the freeze-dried pineapple rings fresh by storing them in an airtight container or resealable bags.

8. Pineapple rings that have been freeze-dried are a tasty and nutritious snack. They're satisfyingly crunchy and have a sweet and sour taste. You may eat them straight up, or you can sprinkle them on top of yogurt, cereal, or dessert.

Keep in mind that the texture and results may change if you attempt to use a home freezer instead of a freeze drier.

These freeze-dried pineapple rings are delicious, and I hope you get to experience them for yourself.

Banana and strawberry freeze-dried snacks

15-minute prep time.
Effort Required: Low

Ingredients
- 1.5 oz. of frozen blueberries
- Bananas, two ripe
- Lemon juice, 1 tablespoon

Instructions

1. Strawberry preparation is a quick rinse with cold water and a little patting with a paper towel. Slice the strawberries thinly and evenly after removing the green tips.

2. Prepare the bananas by peeling them and slicing them into rounds.

3. Squeeze some lemon juice over the strawberry slices and banana rounds and set them in a bowl. Gently toss the fruit pieces in the lemon juice to coat them and keep them from turning brown.

4. Put the fruit slices on the freeze-dryer trays in a single layer. Leave some room for air to circulate between the slices.

5. Follow the freeze dryer's directions for fruit freeze-drying and load the trays inside.

6. Get your freeze dryer going, and let it 12 to 24 hours to dry whatever it is you're trying to preserve, depending on the model and how dry you want it
.

7. Carefully take the strawberry and banana slices from the trays after they are freeze-dried and crisp.

8. Seal the resealable bags or containers airtight and store the freeze-dried strawberry and banana chips inside.

These freeze-dried strawberry and banana chips are a tasty and healthy alternative to regular potato chips. Use them as a snack on their own, in trail mixes, or as a sweet addition to breakfast foods like yogurt and oatmeal.

Keep in mind that the texture and results may change if you use a home dehydrator or a low-temperature oven instead of a freeze drier.

These freeze-dried strawberry and banana chips are delicious, and I hope you love preparing and eating them as much as I do.

Freeze-Dried Chocolatey Treats

Strawberry Chocolate Freeze-Dried Snacks

Ingredients
- Strawberries, freeze-dried, one cup
- 170 grams (6 ounces) of chopped dark or semisweet chocolate
- Sprinkles, crushed almonds, or coconut flakes are some examples of optional toppings.

Time Required for Preparation: Roughly 20 Minutes
Effort Required: Low

Instructions
1. Put some parchment paper on a baking sheet or pan and put it aside.

2. The freeze-dried strawberries should be tossed into a dish and put away.

3. Put a few inches of water in a small saucepan and heat it until it begins to boil. Make sure the bowl's bottom doesn't become wet by placing it on top of the saucepan.

4. Chop some chocolate and toss it into the basin, then whisk it constantly until it melts and becomes smooth. Take the dish away from the stove.

5. Carefully dip each freeze-dried strawberry into the melted chocolate, covering it completely. Let the extra chocolate fall to the side.

6. Put the strawberry with the chocolate coating on the parchment-lined sheet. Use the remaining strawberries in the same way.

7. Before the chocolate hardens, you may sprinkle the strawberries with extra toppings like sprinkles, crushed almonds, or coconut flakes.

8. When you're done coating the strawberries, put the tray in the fridge for at least 15 minutes, or until the chocolate has solidified fully.

9. When the chocolate has hardened, either serve the strawberries right away or store them in an airtight container.

Chocolate-covered freeze-dried strawberries are a gorgeous complement to dessert plates and a wonderful snack all on their own.

Please note that the estimated preparation time may change based on the chef and the state of the kitchen.

Bananas dipped in chocolate and freeze-dried

Time Needed for Preparation: 15
Effort Required: Low
Five servings

Ingredients
- Bananas, freeze-dried: 1 cup
- Chopped or semisweet chocolate (or milk chocolate) that's 6 ounces
- Sprinkles, shredded coconut, toasted coconut flakes, toasted almonds, etc. (as desired)

Instructions
1. Place baking paper on a baking tin or tray.

2. Prepare the chocolate by melting it in a microwave-safe bowl or in a double boiler until it is completely melted and smooth. To melt chocolate in a microwave, heat for 30 seconds at a time and mix well after each heating until melted.

3. To coat the freeze-dried banana slices in chocolate, dip them one at a time into the melted chocolate using a fork or dipping utensil. Let the extra chocolate fall to the side.

4. Transfer the chocolate-covered banana slices to the lined tray, leaving some room between each one. The chocolate will harden correctly if you do this.

5. Banana bits may be dipped in chocolate and then sprinkled with optional toppings while the chocolate is still wet.

6. The banana bits should be chilled in the fridge or freezer for approximately 10 to 15 minutes, or until the chocolate has solidified completely.

7. When the chocolate has hardened, take it out of the fridge or freezer and serve. Peel the banana bits carefully from the parchment paper. They are good to eat right once, or you can preserve them in an airtight container for later.

Enjoy a wonderful snack that combines the best of both worlds with these Chocolate-Dipped Freeze-Dried Banana Bites. Enjoy!

Please note that the amounts may be modified to suit your tastes and the number of people you want to serve.

Rings of freeze-dried apples dipped in chocolate.

The time needed for preparation: 10 minutes
Level of Difficulty: Easy
Five servings

Ingredients
- Apple rings, freeze-dried, one cup
- half a cup of chocolate chips (milk, dark, or white, to taste)

- Sprinkles or chopped nuts as a topping are an option.

Instructions

1. Place baking paper on a baking tin or tray.

2. Put the chocolate chips in a microwave-safe dish and microwave on high until melted. Melt the chocolate in the microwave at 30-second intervals, stirring well after each, until it is fully melted and smooth. The chocolate may also be melted in a double boiler on the stove.

3. To coat the freeze-dried apple rings in chocolate, dip them one at a time using a fork or a dipping tool, and then let the excess chocolate drop off. Coat the apple ring with the coating and place it on the baking sheet. Carry on until all of the apple rings have been used.

4. Use a spoon or a piping bag to pour more melted chocolate in a beautiful pattern over the coated apple rings. Any shape, from zigzags to lines, may be made.

5. As a decorative touch, sprinkle some multicolored sprinkles or chopped nuts on the chocolate drizzle while it is still wet.

6. To solidify the chocolate, chill the baking sheet in the fridge for at least 10 minutes, preferably longer.

7. Once the chocolate has set, gently peel the apple rings off the parchment paper and serve. They are finished and may be eaten as a tasty snack right now. You may

eat them right now, or you can keep them in an airtight container for later.

These freeze-dried apple rings with chocolate dripping are a beautiful and delicious sweet treat. Delight in the contrast of flavors between the freeze-dried apples' crunch and the chocolate's sweetness.

Wedges of freeze-dried pineapple dipped in chocolate

The time needed for preparation: 10 minutes
Hardness: Very Simple
Five servings

Ingredients
- One cup of frozen pineapple chunks
- chocolate, milk, dark, or semisweet, 8 ounces (225 grams), chopped
- Sprinkles, crushed almonds, or shredded coconut may be used as a topping.

Instructions
1. Place baking paper on a baking tin or tray.

2. Chop up some chocolate and put it in a microwave-safe basin to melt. Melt the chocolate in the microwave at 30-second intervals, stirring after each, until it is completely smooth. You may also use a double boiler on the stovetop to melt the chocolate.

3. To coat the freeze-dried pineapple wedges in chocolate, dip them into the melted chocolate using a fork or a tiny set of tongs. Let the extra chocolate fall to the side.

4. Carefully move the chocolate-covered pineapple wedge to the lined tray, spreading it out so that there is some room between each one. The remaining pineapple wedges should be treated in the same manner.

5. Sprinkles, crushed almonds, or coconut flakes may be added to the wet chocolate coating on the pineapple wedges before serving.

6. Put the tray in the fridge for 15 to 20 minutes, or until the chocolate has firmed, to allow it to set.

7. When the chocolate has hardened, take it out of the fridge and serve. Now you can eat chocolate-covered freeze-dried pineapple wedges. They are best served right away but may be kept in an airtight container for up to three days at room temperature.

You'll love the sweet and sour taste of these freeze-dried pineapple wedges covered in chocolate. You may eat them by yourself or as an attractive addition to dessert trays.

Raspberry Clusters Covered in Chocolate That Have Been Freeze-Dried

Ten-Minute Preparation Time
Hardness: Very Simple

Ingredients
- Raspberry powder, 1 cup freeze-dried
- Chopped chocolate (dark, milk, or white, 6 ounces/ 170 grams)

Instructions
1. Get out a baking sheet and line it with a silicone mat or parchment paper.

2. Chop the chocolate bar into small pieces and place it in a microwave-safe dish. Microwave on high for 30 seconds at a time, stirring carefully after each, until the chocolate is completely melted and smooth. Alternatively, you may use a double boiler over a pot of boiling water to melt the chocolate, being careful that the bottom of the bowl doesn't contact the water.

3. To the melted chocolate, add the freeze-dried raspberries and mix gently until the berries are evenly covered.

4. Drop clumps of the chocolate-covered raspberries onto the prepared baking sheet using a spoon or a tiny cookie scoop. If you like, you may make the clusters as big or as little as you like.

5. Allow the clusters to rest for 15–20 minutes at room temperature so the chocolate may harden. Alternatively, you may chill the baking sheet in the fridge to speed up the setting process.

6. The Raspberry Clusters may be eaten as soon as the chocolate has set. You may eat them right once, or keep them in an airtight jar for up to a week at room temperature.

Enjoy the perfect balance of sweet chocolate and tangy raspberries in these freeze-dried raspberry clusters coated in chocolate. They are a quick and simple way to satisfy your sweet tooth. Enjoy!

Freeze-dried peaches dipped in chocolate

Ingredients
- 2.25 ounces of peach slices, freeze-dried
- Eight ounces of chopped chocolate (milk, dark, or white)
- Toppings like almonds, coconut, and sprinkles are optional.

15-minute prep time.
Hardness: Very Simple

Instructions
1. Line a baking tin with baking paper and have it ready to go.

2. To melt chocolate, put pieces in a microwave-safe basin. Melt the chocolate in the microwave in 30-second increments, stirring after each, until it is completely melted and smooth. You may also use a double boiler on the stovetop to melt the chocolate.

3. Coat the freeze-dried peach slices well in melted chocolate by dipping them one at a time. Remove any extra chocolate from the peach slice by lifting it with a fork or dipping utensil.

4. Transfer the peach slice that has been covered in chocolate to the baking sheet. The remaining peach slices should be treated in the same manner.

5. Sprinkle toppings on the chocolate-coated peach slices while the chocolate is still wet if desired. Possible toppings include chopped almonds, shredded coconut, and sprinkles.

6. Put the baking sheet in the fridge or on a cool counter until the chocolate coating has a firm, whichever comes first. About fifteen to twenty minutes is about average for this.

7. When the chocolate has hardened, the freeze-dried peaches with chocolate coating are ready to be served and stored. Use them as a side dish or a sweet treat. Any leftovers may be kept for up to a week at room temperature in an airtight container.

This dish is a great way to savor freeze-dried peaches that have been covered in chocolate. Enjoy your time in the kitchen with these tasty goodies.

Clusters of freeze-dried raspberry and pistachio nuts dipped in chocolate

Time Needed for Preparation: 15
Effort Required: Low

Ingredients
- Raspberry powder, 1 cup freeze-dried
- Shelled pistachios, 1/2 cup
- 8 ounces of unsweetened chocolate, in chunks or chips.
- The use of parchment

Instructions
1. Prepare a baking tray by lining it with baking paper.

2. Freeze-dried raspberries and shelled pistachios should be mixed together in a dish. Blend them together carefully to achieve equilibrium.

3. Dark chocolate should be warmed in a microwave-safe dish or over a double boiler until smooth and melted. Regular stirring is necessary to guarantee uniform melting.

4. Remove the chocolate from the fire and set it aside to cool for a few minutes after it has melted.

5. Melt the chocolate and add it to the dish of raspberries and nuts. Mix slowly so that everything is equally coated.

6. Drop the mixture by a spoonful or with a tiny cookie scoop onto the lined baking sheet. Produce groups with diameters of a single inch to two.

7. To solidify the chocolate, refrigerate or freeze the baking sheet containing the clusters. This normally takes about twenty to thirty minutes.

8. When the clusters have solidified completely, take them out of the fridge or freezer.

9. Enjoy the chocolate-covered freeze-dried raspberry and pistachio clusters as soon as possible, or keep them in an airtight container in a cold, dry location.

These clusters are a delightfully crunchy snack, with a taste profile that strikes the ideal mix between sweet, sour, and nutty. Enjoy!

Please keep in mind that cooking times may vary based on how quickly and how precisely each person prepares their food. Recipe modifications are possible to accommodate special diets and individual tastes.

Pina Colada and Macadamia Nut Bites, Freeze-Dried, and Covered in Chocolate

15-minute prep time.
Effort Required: Low
Five servings

Ingredients

- One cup of frozen pineapple pieces
- Macadamia nuts, 1/2 cup
- chocolate, milk, dark, or semisweet, 6 ounces, chopped
- Coconut shreds are an optional topping.

Instructions

1. Line a baking sheet with parchment paper and have it ready for use.

2. The chopped chocolate may be heated in the microwave in 30-second increments, stirred in between, until it is completely melted and smooth, in a microwave-safe bowl. You may also use a double boiler on the stovetop to melt the chocolate.

3. Put a macadamia nut in the middle of a piece of freeze-dried pineapple. Toss the remaining macadamia nuts and pineapple pieces for a second time.

4. Carefully dip each pineapple and macadamia nut bite into the melted chocolate, using a fork or dipping

utensil, to ensure a complete coating. Let the extra chocolate fall to the side.

5. Transfer the doused nuggets to the baking sheet. Before the chocolate hardens, you may add some shredded coconut on top of each mouthful if you want.

6. Continue dipping the pineapple and macadamia nut bits until they are all covered with chocolate.

7. To set the chocolate, chill the baking sheet with the coated bits in the fridge for 15–20 minutes.

8. Once the chocolate has hardened, take the bits out of the fridge and place them on a serving platter or in an airtight container.

9. As a snack or dessert, serve and enjoy these freeze-dried pineapple and macadamia nut bites covered in chocolate.

Pineapple, macadamia nuts, and chocolate come together in perfect harmony in these bite-sized morsels. If you're in the mood for something sweet and crunchy, these are it. Enjoy!

Bars made of freeze-dried fruits and nuts

Bars with Almonds and Freeze-Dried Berries

15-minute prep time.
Effort Required: Low
Five servings

Ingredients
- 1 cup of freeze-dried mixed berries; may use whatever combination of berries you choose.
- 1/3 pound almonds
- 12 cups of oats, rolled
- 1/4 cup of maple syrup or honey
- Almond butter,25 cup
- Extract Vanilla, 14 Teaspoon
- A dollop of salt

Instructions
1. The freeze-dried berries may be coarsely mashed by pulsing them in a food processor or blender. Remove from consideration.

2. The almonds may be processed in the same blender or food processor to get a similar gritty texture. Look out to avoid over-process; you want to keep some consistency. Put the almond pieces in a large basin.

3. Put the oats in the same bowl as the almonds.

4. Honey or maple syrup, almond butter, vanilla essence, and a pinch of salt should be warmed over low heat in a small pot. Blend together and smooth out with a good stir.

5. Warm the mixture and pour it over the oat and almonds in the bowl. Mix in some freeze-dried berry powder. Make sure everything is equally covered and mixed by mixing it well.

6. Prepare a parchment paper-lined square baking dish. Put the mixture in the dish and pack it down evenly and firmly with your hands or the back of a spoon.

7. Let the dish sit in the fridge for at least 2 hours, or until firm.

8. When ready, use the parchment paper's edges to lift the mixture out of the dish. To customize the size, slice it into bars or squares.

9. Have fun eating! The bars can keep in the fridge for up to a week if stored in an airtight container.

Crunchy almonds, chewy oats, and the delicious taste of freeze-dried berries come together in perfect harmony in these Freeze-Dried berries and Almond Bars. They are a quick and healthful choice for a snack.

I trust you will have fun whipping up these tasty treats with this recipe.

Tropical Fruit and Macadamia Nut Bars, Freeze-Dried

15-minute prep time.
Effort Required: Low
Five bars per serving.

Ingredients

- 1 cup of freeze-dried tropic fruit (strawberries, bananas, etc.)
- Macadamia nuts, 1 cup, unsalted
- 1 cup of pitted dates
- 14 cups of coconut flakes
- 1/4 cup of maple syrup or honey
- Vanilla extract, half a teaspoon
- A dollop of salt

Instructions

1. Pulse the freeze-dried tropical fruit combination in a food processor until it resembles tiny chunks.

2. The dates and macadamia nuts should be placed in a food processor. Maintain processing until a cohesive mass forms from the combination.

3. Shredded coconut, honey/maple syrup, vanilla essence, and a dash of salt should be placed in a food processor and blended until smooth. Repeat the

process until all of the ingredients are evenly distributed and the mixture is cohesive.

4. Use parchment paper to line a baking dish or pan, providing an overhang for subsequent removal.

5. Put the contents of the food processor onto the ready baking dish. Compact the layer by pressing down evenly and firmly.

6. For best results, chill the meal in the fridge for at least 2 hours.

7. After the ingredients have had time to cool and firm up, pull the parchment paper out of the baking dish and remove the mixture.

8. Cut the mixture into bars of the appropriate size using a sharp knife.

9. Store the bars in an airtight container or individually wrap them in parchment paper.

Sweet tropical tastes and crunchy macadamia nuts come together in perfect harmony in these freeze-dried bars. They are a great option for a quick and nutritious snack on the run.

Put those homemade freeze-dried bars to good use.

Apple Walnut Freeze-Dried Bars

Ingredients

- apples, freeze-dried, 2 cups
- 1/2 lb. almonds
- 1 cup of pitted dates
- Just a quarter of a cup of honey
- Vanilla extract, 1 teaspoon
- A Half-Teaspoon of Cinnamon Powder
- A dollop of salt

Preparation

1. The freeze-dried apples and walnuts are coarsely ground in a food processor.

2. Put the dates in a food processor along with the honey, vanilla, cinnamon, and salt. Repeat pulsing until the ingredients start to adhere together and form a dough.

3. Prepare a parchment paper-lined baking sheet or dish.

4. Spread the mixture equally in the prepared baking dish and push down hard to compress it.

5. To put the mixture in the dish, refrigerate it for at least 2 hours.

6. When ready, take the mixture out of the fridge and divide it into bars or squares of whatever size you choose.

You may eat it right away or put it in the fridge in an airtight container for later.

About 15 minutes are needed for preparation.

Effort Required: Low

About 5 bars of freeze-dried apple and walnut goodness may be made with this recipe. Enjoy!

Mango Cashew Freeze-Dried Bars

15-minute prep time.
Effort Required: Low
Five bars per serving.

Ingredients
- One cup of frozen mango chunks
- Cashews, one cup
- 1 cup of pitted dates
- 2 tablespoons sweetener, such as honey or maple syrup
- Optional Flavoring: 1/4 Teaspoon Vanilla Extract

Instructions
1. Put the cashews and freeze-dried mango chunks in a food processor. Pulse them until they are finely chopped, like coarse crumbs.

2. Put the dates with the pits in the food processor and run them until the ingredients start to cling together.

3. To sweeten and flavor the mixture, you may add honey or maple syrup and vanilla essence. Repeat the pulsing process a few more times to ensure thorough mixing.

4. Prepare a parchment paper lining for a square baking dish or other container. Spread the mixture evenly after transferring it to the dish. Compact the ingredients by pressing down hard.

5. For best results, chill the dish in the fridge for at least an hour.

6. When the mixture has been set, take it from the dish and cut it into bars of the appropriate size.

7. The bars made from freeze-dried mango and cashews may be kept in the fridge for up to two weeks if stored in an airtight container.

Mango and cashews complement each other well in these bars. They're delicious and nutritious, so you can eat them whenever you want.

Please note that you may change the amount of sugar or other flavors to your liking. To make the bars more to your preference, you may play around with adding things like shredded coconut or spices. Enjoy!

Bars with Pistachios and Freeze-Dried Apricots

Ingredients
- Frozen apricots, one cup
- 1 cup of shelled pistachios
- 1 cup of pitted dates
- Depending on your preference, use 1/4 cup honey or maple syrup.
- Vanilla extract, half a teaspoon
- A dollop of salt

Time Needed to Get Ready: Roughly 15
Effort Required: Low

Instructions
1. Put the freeze-dried fruit, nuts, sweetener, vanilla, and a little salt into a food processor.

2. Mix all the ingredients in a food processor until they form a sticky dough. It's possible that you'll need to pause periodically to scrape down the edges of the food processor bowl.

3. When everything is mixed together, put it in a skillet or dish that has been covered with foil. Evenly and firmly press it down with your palms or the back of a spoon.

4. Refrigerate the dish or pan for at least an hour, preferably two, to solidify the mixture.

5. Once the mixture has set, you may take it from the dish and slice it into bars or other shapes.

6. The freeze-dried apricot and pistachio snacks may be served right away or stored in the fridge in an airtight container. You may take pleasure in them for many days.

The sweet and salty tastes of these freeze-dried apricot and pistachio snacks are a match made in heaven. They are great for a quick bite on the run or as a healthy dessert option. Enjoy!

Please be aware that this recipe is rather simple and will make enough for around 5 people. If you want to make fewer or more servings, feel free to change the proportions.

Pecan and Cranberry Bars

Ingredients
- Cranberries, freeze-dried, one cup
- Chopped pecans to the tune of 1 cup
- 1 cup of oats, rolled
- Almond butter, half a cup
- Just a quarter of a cup of honey
- Sugar Maple Syrup, 1/4 Cup
- Vanilla extract, 1 teaspoon
- A Pinch of Salt, Only

Instructions
1. Freeze-dried cranberries, pecan pieces, rolled oats, and salt should all be mixed together in a big basin.

Combine well so that everything is equally distributed.

2. Almond butter, honey, maple syrup, and vanilla extract should be heated separately in a microwave-safe bowl. Stirring after each 30-second microwave interval, continue this process until the liquid is completely melted and smooth.

3. Put the dry ingredients in a bowl and pour the almond butter mixture over them. The mixture is ready when it turns sticky after being stirred and all the ingredients have been coated.

4. Use parchment paper to line a baking sheet. Put the mixture into the pan and push it down hard to level it out.

5. Chill the pan in the fridge for at least 2 hours, or until the bars have set.

6. The bars are ready to be removed from the pan and cut into squares or bars after they have hardened.

Have fun eating! These bars keep well in the fridge for up to two weeks if kept in an airtight container.

About 15 minutes are needed for preparation.
Effort Required: Low

This Freeze-Dried Cranberry and Pecan Bars recipe makes around 5 bars. You may change the amounts to suit your needs.

Inventive New Flavors of Freeze-Dried Sweets

Watermelon gummy bears that have been frozen solid

Ingredients
- Watermelon freeze-dried bits, 1 cup
- Sugar, Granulated, 1 Cup
- Thin corn syrup, 1/3 cup
- 1-fourth of a cup of water
- Candy sticks

Instructions
1. Put the freeze-dried watermelon chunks in a blender or food processor. Pulse them until they become a powder. Remove from consideration.

2. Use parchment paper or a silicone mat to line a baking sheet. Place lollipop sticks onto the baking sheet, making sure there is enough room for each one to set without touching.

3. Mix the granulated sugar, light corn syrup, and water in a small saucepan. The sugar should dissolve fully as you stir it over medium heat.

4. Bring the mixture to a simmer over a moderate-high heat. Put a candy thermometer into the pot, and keep

boiling until the mixture reaches the hard crack stage, at around 300 degrees Fahrenheit (149 degrees Celsius).

5. Take the pan from the stove and wait for the bubbling to stop. Let the mixture sit for a few minutes until it thickens just enough to be pourable.

6. Spoon the melted sugar mixture into a tiny circle at the end of each lollipop stick. Before the sugar sets, sprinkle a little of the freeze-dried watermelon powder on each lollipop.

7. Please wait until the lollipops have fully hardened at room temperature. Carefully lift them from the baking sheet after they have set.

8. Watermelon lollipops that have been freeze-dried should be kept in an airtight container or individually wrapped in plastic wrap to maintain their flavor and freshness.

These watermelon lollipops are freeze-dried for a concentrated taste that is both unusual and pleasant. This unique candy is a perfect blend of sugary sweetness and juicy taste.

Sugary Drops Made from Freeze-Dried Fruits

15-minute prep time.
Level of Difficulty: Easy
Five servings

Ingredients
- a couple of huge oranges, lemons, or limes
- 1 tbsp sugar (not required)

Instructions
1. It is recommended that you pre-heat your freeze dryer before using it for the first time.

2. Remove any debris or wax from the citrus fruits by washing them under running water. Use a kitchen paper to dab them.

3. Cut the citrus fruits into uniformly thin slices, no thicker than a quarter of an inch. If possible, take out the seeds.

4. Sugar may be sprinkled on the citrus slices to increase their sweetness. If you like a more tart taste, you may omit this step.

5. Place the citrus slices on the trays or racks of the freeze dryer, being sure to leave some room between each one so that air can circulate freely.

6. Put the trays or racks into the freeze drier and activate the drying cycle specified in the manual. The ideal temperature and drying time may vary based on the make and type of your freeze drier.

7. The citrus slices may be freeze-dried entirely if you let the freeze-drier take its course. Please be patient with the procedure as it may take many hours.

8. After the citrus fruit drops have been freeze-dried, the trays or racks may be taken out of the freeze-dried and allowed to cool to room temperature.

9. Put the freeze-dried citrus fruit drops in a sealed bag or airtight container. Keep them in a dry, dark area out of the reach of dampness and heat.

These freeze-dried citrus fruit drops are a delicious and tangy snack that can also be used as a garnish for sweets, savory dishes, and drinks.

The natural tastes of citrus fruits are preserved in a crisp and light form in these freeze-dried citrus fruit drops, making them a wonderful and one-of-a-kind snack. Savor the tangy flavor of them!

Please keep in mind that the freeze dryer type and the thickness of the citrus slices will determine the drying duration and temperature. If you want to get the greatest results, follow the manufacturer's guidelines.

Candy made from a blend of frozen fruits

Get ready in under 15 minutes.
Level of Difficulty: Easy
5 portions are provided.

Ingredients
- Mixed fruits (strawberries, blueberries, and raspberries) freeze-dried to make 1 cup
- A Half Cup Of Water
- Honey or maple syrup, 2 teaspoons
- 2 teaspoons of gelatin

Instructions
1. Use a blender or food processor to reduce the freeze-dried fruit mixture to a powder. Remove from consideration.

2. Put the water and gelatin powder in a small saucepan and bring to a boil. After 5 minutes, the gelatin should be ready to use.

3. Heat the mixture in a saucepan over low heat, stirring often, until the gelatin is dissolved. The blend should not be brought to a simmer.

4. To the pot, add the honey or maple syrup and swirl to combine.

5. Turn off the stove and stir in the freeze-dried mixed fruit powder after it has been pulverized. Make sure there are no lumps by stirring vigorously.

6. The mixture may be poured into a square baking dish coated with parchment paper or silicone candy molds.

7. Put the mixture in the fridge after letting it cool for approximately 30 minutes at room temperature. Wait at least two hours, or until it's firm.

8. Once the gummies have been set, you may take them out of the molds or use a baking dish to cut them into the appropriate shapes.

9. You may keep the freeze-dried mixed fruit gummies in the fridge for up to a week if you put them in an airtight container.

Treat yourself to a tasty and nutritious snack with these freeze-dried mixed fruit gummies.

Fruit Bark That Has Been Frozen

Ten-Minute Preparation Time
Effort Required: Low
Five servings

Ingredients
- 2 cups of freeze-dried fruit (any combination of berries and/or mangoes).
- 8 ounces of melted chocolate, either dark or milk
- Almonds or pistachios, chopped (optional, 2 teaspoons)

Instructions

1. Get out a baking sheet and line it with a silicone mat or parchment paper.

2. Use your hands or a rolling pin to crush the freeze-dried fruits into smaller bits in a basin. Keep some chunks intact for textural variety.

3. Use a microwave-safe bowl to melt the chocolate, stirring every 30 seconds until it is completely melted and smooth.

4. Spread the melted chocolate out in a thin layer on the prepared baking sheet using a spatula.

5. The broken freeze-dried fruits should be sprinkled over the melted chocolate right away, and then gently pressed into the chocolate to help them stick.

6. Chopped nuts may be sprinkled on the chocolate and fruit if you choose.

7. If you want the chocolate to be extra hard, you may chill the baking sheet in the fridge for 30 minutes.

8. When the bark has dried, cut it up with your hands or a knife to make smaller, more random pieces.

9. The freeze-dried fruit bark may be kept for up to two weeks if stored in an airtight container in the refrigerator.

You and your loved ones will like this bright and tasty freeze-dried fruit bark very much.

Both the estimated cooking time and the estimated degree of difficulty are subject to change based on the chef and the tools at their disposal.

Energy Balls Made From Freeze-Dried Fruit And Nuts

15-minute prep time.
Hardness: Very Simple
Five servings

Ingredients

- 1 cup of freeze-dried berries (strawberries, blueberries, or a combination)
- 1 cup of chopped nuts (pecans, almonds, cashews, etc.)
- 1 cup of pitted dates
- 2 tablespoons of any kind of nut butter (like peanut or almond butter).
- 1 tablespoon of honey or maple syrup (to savor)
- Vanilla extract, half a teaspoon
- A Pinch of Salt, Only
- Extra freeze-dried fruit or nuts to use as a coating (if desired).

Instructions

1. The freeze-dried fruit and nuts should be coarsely minced in a food processor. Put the blend in a bowl and place aside.

2. The dates, nut butter, honey/maple syrup (if used), vanilla extract, and salt should all go into the same food processor. Blend until a sticky dough forms.

3. To the dough in the food processor, add the freeze-dried fruit and nut combination that has been chopped. Just give it a little whirl to mix everything together.

4. Roll a tiny amount of the mixture between your hands to make a ball. To add a coating, you may roll the balls in crushed freeze-dried fruit or nuts.

5. Energy balls should be refrigerated for at least 30 minutes to harden, either on a baking sheet or in an airtight container.

6. Freeze-dried fruit and nut energy balls may be eaten after being refrigerated. They may be kept for up to a week in the fridge.

Dates and freeze-dried fruit provide a natural sweetness, while the energy-boosting benefits of almonds round out this snack. They are a great choice for a quick and nutritious midday pick-me-up.

Please use your favorite freeze-dried fruit and nut combination to tailor the recipe to your tastes. For a different taste and texture, try adding some chia seeds, coconut flakes, or cocoa powder.

The Freeze-Dried Fruit and Nut Energy Balls are a delight to make and eat.

Freeze-Dried Sweets for Special Occasions

Strawberry Hearts, Freeze Dried

15-minute prep time.
Effort Required: Low
Five servings

Ingredients
- Strawberries, freeze-dried, one cup
- Decorative white chocolate chips, 1/4 cup

Instructions
1. Blend or process the freeze-dried strawberries. Pulse them until they become a powder. Remove from consideration.

2. Get out some parchment paper or a silicone baking mat and set up a baking sheet.

3. Set the oven temperature to its lowest possible setting, typically 170 degrees Fahrenheit or 75 degrees Celsius.

4. Use a cookie cutter in the form of a heart to make cookies on the ready baking sheet.

5. Spread the freeze-dried strawberry powder around the cookie cutter until it completely fills the form. Use the back of the ladle to softly push it down.

6. Lift the cookie cutter carefully to reveal a heart-shaped slice of freeze-dried strawberry. Do this 4 more times to make 5 strawberry heart shapes.

7. Put the strawberry hearts on a baking sheet and into the hot oven. To speed up the drying process, crack the oven door open a crack. This will aid in the crisping of the hearts.

8. For dry and crispy strawberry hearts, bake at 300 degrees for 1 to 1.5 hours. Cooking time will vary according to oven temperature and heart thickness. Always keep a close watch on fire hazards.

9. Take the hearts out of the oven when they are dry and allow them to cool on the baking sheet.

10. White chocolate chip melting is entirely up to personal preference. White chocolate should be melted and drizzled over the cooled strawberry hearts for decoration.

11. The strawberry hearts should rest for a while to let the chocolate harden before being served or stored.

These freeze-dried strawberry hearts are delicious on their own or as a beautiful topping for ice cream, cakes, or cupcakes. They make great presents or may be enjoyed on their own.

Keep in mind that you may keep the freeze-dried strawberry hearts at room temperature for up to a week if you store them in an airtight container.

Banana Spirits (Halloween) - Freeze Dried

Ten-Minute Preparation Time
Hardness: Very Simple

Ingredients
- Five perfectly ripe bananas
- Ingredients: candy melts or white chocolate chips
- To make the eyes, use either little chocolate chips or chocolate sprinkles.
- Skewers or popsicle sticks (not required)

Instructions
1. Bananas should be peeled and then halved lengthwise. Popsicle sticks or skewers may be used to make handles by inserting them into the open end of each banana half.

2. The bananas should be cut in half and then placed on a baking pan either with parchment paper or a silicone mat.

3. White chocolate may be melted from chips or candy melts using the procedures provided. Make sure the chocolate has fully melted and is smooth.

4. Spread the melted white chocolate over each banana half, covering it completely, using a spoon or a tiny spatula. To make a ghost, just cut off the banana so that the bottom is visible, creating a "ghost tail."

5. Press two small chocolate chips or chocolate sprinkles into each banana half while the white chocolate is still wet to make the ghost's eyes. If you need more help sticking the eyeballs on, you may add melted white chocolate as an adhesive.

6. Use this method with the remaining banana halves.

7. To ensure the white chocolate is completely set, place the baking sheet with the banana ghosts in the freezer for at least 2 hours.

8. After the banana ghosts have frozen, store them in an airtight container or enjoy them right away.

Treat yourself this Halloween with these creepy and tasty Freeze-Dried Banana Ghosts. You can count on them to be the talk of every Halloween party you attend.

Keep in mind that you may get a similar result by freezing the banana ghosts on a baking sheet until the white chocolate solidifies if you don't have access to a freeze drier. However, freeze-drying gives the bananas their greatest texture and keeps them fresh for a longer period of time.

These Freeze-Dried Banana Ghosts should be fun to make. If you have any further research, please inform me through your review.

Apple stars, freeze-dried for the 4th of July

Ten-Minute Preparation Time
Effort Required: Low
Five servings

Ingredients
- Double-size Apples
- Extract one lemon
- Coloring agents (gel or powder) in the colors red, white, and blue.
- Drizzle of honey or maple syrup (to savor)

Instructions
1. Apples should be washed and stickers removed before being sliced. Thinly slice the apples across the width into horizontal strips. Remove the center and throw it away.

2. To keep apple slices from turning brown, give them a quick dip in a bath of fresh lemon juice. Make sure the slices are evenly covered with lemon juice by giving them a little toss.

3. Divide the apple slices into thirds and color each third a different color. Three bowls should be prepared: one with a few drops of red food coloring, one with a few

drops of blue food coloring, and one left white. Roll the apple slices around in each dish to get a good coating of color.

4. Apple slices should be freeze-dried in a single layer without overlapping, so place them on freeze-drying trays or a prepared baking sheet. To freeze the food, either use a freeze drier or put the trays in the freezer. To get perfectly dry and crisp slices, either use a freeze dryer according to the manufacturer's directions or freeze them for around 24 hours.

5. Arrange the Stars Take the freeze-dried apple slices out of the freezer or freeze drier. The colorful apple slices may be used as a stencil for a star-shaped cookie cutter. If a star-shaped cookie cutter is unavailable, you may alternatively use a knife to cut out the shapes by hand.

6. Drizzle Optional: For an extra sweet touch, you may drizzle a little bit of honey or maple syrup over the freeze-dried apple stars. If you apply too much, the stars will get stuck.

7. Put the Freeze-Dried Apple Stars on a tray for guests or give them out in snack packs. You may now serve them as a patriotic dessert at your July 4th party!

These Freeze-Dried Apple Stars are an eye-catching snack that also happens to be tasty and nutritious. As you enjoy the season, savor their crisp texture and brilliant hues. Have a wonderful Independence Day!

Pineapple flower petals (Spring/Easter) – freeze-dried

Ten-Minute Preparation Time
Effort Required: Low
Five servings

Ingredients
- ONE BRAND-NEW PINEAPPLE
- Optional (for color retention) lemon juice.

Instructions
1. Peel the pineapple and cut off the top to have it ready to use. Crosswise rounds of pineapple about 14 in (6 mm) thick are called for.

2. If you want to keep the pineapple's natural color as it dries, you may dip each slice in lemon juice. This is totally discretionary.

3. Spread the pineapple slices out in a single layer on the freeze dryer's trays, making sure they don't touch.

4. Put the trays into the freeze drier and adjust the settings for freeze-drying fruits as directed by the manufacturer. This is done by commencing the freeze-drying process at a temperature of around 0 degrees Fahrenheit (-18 degrees Celsius).

5. You should freeze-dry the pineapple slices for the time specified. Pineapple drying time might vary based on the freeze drier type and the pineapple

slices' thickness. If you want to get the most out of it, do what the manufacturer suggests.

6. After the pineapple slices have been freeze-dried, take them out of the freeze-dried and allow them cool to room temperature.

7. To remove the freeze-dried pineapple slices from the trays, use caution. They ought to be fresh and light, like blossoms.

8. Protect the freshness and taste of your freeze-dried pineapple blossoms by storing them in an airtight container or bag.

Delicious and unusual, these freeze-dried pineapple blossoms are a great addition to any Spring or Easter celebration. They're great as a standalone healthful snack or sprinkled on yogurt or ice cream for a sweet treat. These freeze-dried pineapple blooms are as beautiful as they are tasty.

Keep in mind that the drying time will vary depending on variables like the pineapple slices' thickness and the effectiveness of your freeze drier. If you want to know the exact instructions for using your freeze dryer, look in the handbook.

Winter/Christmas Freeze-Dried Blueberry Snowflakes

Ingredients
- 2 cups of blueberries, freeze-dried
- 1-fourth cup of powdered sugar
- Lemon juice, 1 tablespoon
- Vanilla extract, half a teaspoon

Instructions
1. Throw the freeze-dried blueberries into a blender or food processor. Pulse them until they become a powdery consistency.

2. Mix the dried blueberries, sugar, lemon juice, and vanilla essence together in a bowl. To ensure that all of the components are uniformly distributed, mix them well.

3. The finished product should have the texture of a somewhat sticky dough. If the texture is off, try adding a splash of lemon juice or water.

4. Place the ball of dough on a clean, floured work surface.

5. With a rolling pin, make the batter flatten to a density of approximately 1/2 inch.

6. Cut out snowflake forms from the dough using cookie cutters of the appropriate shape. Arrange the

snowflakes on a baking sheet coated with parchment paper.

7. To consume the batter, just redo the steps.

8. Put the baking sheet in the freezer for at least an hour, or until the snowflakes are solid.

9. The snowflakes may be kept in an airtight container or freeze-drying bags after they have been frozen.

10. You can make it seem even snowier by sprinkling more powdered sugar on top of the snowflakes.

The blueberry snowflakes may be eaten as is or used as a festive edible decoration for cakes, cupcakes, or other sweets.

The time needed for preparation: around 15 minutes
Level of Difficulty: Easy

There are 5 servings in this recipe, but you may easily create more or less snowflakes by changing the proportions. These freeze-dried blueberry snowflakes are a delicious addition to any winter or holiday party.

Valentine's Day Freeze-Dried Raspberry Cupid Arrows

Ingredients
- Raspberry powder, 1 cup freeze-dried
- Candy melts or white chocolate chips, 1 cup
- Lollipop sticks or bamboo skewers
- Ribbon, optionally red or pink

Instructions
1. Blend or process the freeze-dried raspberries until smooth. Pulse them until they become a powdery consistency.

2. White chocolate may be melted in the microwave in a dish as directed on the bag. Reconstitute it until it's melted and smooth.

3. Insert a bamboo skewer or lollipop stick into a pile of freeze-dried raspberry powder that has been dunked in melted white chocolate. If you sprinkle some raspberry powder on top of the chocolate, you can make an arrowhead form.

4. Make sure to leave enough room at the other end of each skewer or stick to use as a handle, and then repeat with the rest.

5. Skewer or stick the raspberries and set them on a parchment-lined baking tray to cool and solidify the chocolate.

6. Add some flair by tying a red or pink ribbon around the end of the handle on each arrow.

The arrows may be served or used as edible decorations after they have cooled and hardened.

The time needed for preparation: around 15 minutes
Level of Difficulty: Easy

You may easily produce more or fewer Cupid arrows by adjusting the ingredients in this recipe. These freeze-dried raspberry Cupid arrows are a delicious holiday treat or thoughtful present for the ones you love.

Orange Halloween Pumpkins, Dried and Freeze-Dried

Ingredients
- Five hefty oranges
- Sugar, Granulated, 1 Cup
- Orange flavoring (not required).
- Green sugar melts or piping gel for pumpkin stems.

Instructions
1. Remove the oranges' tops to use as covers. Please put the tops aside.

2. Carefully use a spoon or melon baller to remove the oranges' meat without puncturing the skin. The orange meat should be saved for later.

3. Mix the granulated sugar and orange food coloring (if using) in a large bowl. Blend well to disperse the hue evenly.

4. Empty orange halves into the basin containing the colored sugar. Tap off any excess sugar before rolling each orange shell in the sugar.

5. Put the orange shells, which you've sprinkled with sugar, on a baking sheet lined with parchment paper and freeze them (or put them in the freezer, if you don't have a freeze drier). Put them in the freezer for at least 4 hours, or until they are well frozen and dry.

6. Take the orange husks out of the freezer or freeze the drier after they have dried out.

7. Make pumpkin stems for the top of each orange shell by piping green piping gel or melting green sugar melts. Give the stems some time to stiffen.

8. To make pumpkins, replace the tops on each orange container.

The orange pumpkins, which have been freeze-dried, may be used as a spectacular Halloween treat or as table decorations.

Time to prepare: around 15 minutes (plus chilling).
Level of Difficulty: Easy

This recipe yields 5 servings of freeze-dried orange pumpkins, but the amounts may easily be changed to create more or less. These pumpkins are both cute and tasty, perfect for celebrating Halloween.

Shamrocks made from freeze-dried lemons for St. Patrick's Day.

Ingredients
- To wit: 2 big lemons
- Sugar, Granulated, 1/4 Cup
- Green food coloring may be used instead.

Instructions
1. Set the oven temperature to its lowest possible setting, typically 170 degrees Fahrenheit or 75 degrees Celsius.

2. Lemons should be washed thoroughly to eliminate any residue or debris.

3. Cut the lemons into uniform rounds using a sharp knife.

4. Spread the lemon slices out in a single layer on a baking sheet covered with parchment paper.

5. Coat the lemon slices with granulated sugar. If you want to make them more Christmassy, you may add some green food coloring.

6. Dry out the lemon slices for around 2 to 3 hours in a preheated oven on a baking sheet. To ensure they dry evenly, check on them often and flip the oven sheet.

7. It's important to keep checking the lemon slices to make sure they've dried out and become crisp. They shouldn't be tacky or wet in the slightest.

8. After the lemon slices have dried completely, take them out of the oven and set them somewhere cold.

9. To make shamrocks out of the dried lemon slices, use a tiny shamrock-shaped cookie cutter.

10. Keep the freeze-dried lemon shamrocks in a sealed freezer bag or airtight container until ready to use.

The freeze-dried lemon shamrocks may be served as a snack on St. Patrick's Day or used as a garnish for baked goods.

The time needed for cooking is around 2 to 3 hours (not including chilling time).
Level of Difficulty: Easy

You may easily produce fewer or more freeze-dried lemon shamrocks by adjusting the ingredients in this recipe. These St. Patrick's Day snacks in the form of shamrocks are delicious.

Springtime Cherry Blossoms, Dried and Freeze-Packed

Ingredients

- Edible and pesticide-free fresh cherry blossoms.
- Sugar, Granulated, 1/4 Cup
- Meringue powder, one tablespoon (optional; adds stability).

Instructions

1. To remove any dirt or debris from the fresh cherry blossoms, just rinse them in cold water. Use a kitchen paper to dab them.

2. Mix the meringue powder (if using) with the granulated sugar in a small bowl.

3. Coat each cherry blossom with sugar by dipping it in the mixture and turning it over. Remove any surplus sugar by shaking.

4. Coat the cherry blossoms and set them on a wire rack or parchment paper.

5. Prepare a low-speed fan or dehydrator. To dry the cherry blossoms, set up a drying rack in front of a fan or put them in a dehydrator and let them be there for 24 to 48 hours. Depending on the relative humidity where you are, the drying time might be different.

6. Make sure the cherry blossoms are drying uniformly by checking on them at regular intervals. When properly dried, they should become crisp and brittle.

7. When the cherry blossoms are dry, take them off the baking sheet or wire rack.

8. To preserve their quality, freeze-dried cherry blossoms should be kept in an airtight container in a cold, dry area.

About 15 minutes is all it takes to have everything ready (not including drying time).
Level of difficulty: moderate

Take care to only utilize cherry blossoms that have not been treated with any harmful chemicals or pesticides. Also, make sure the flowers are of good quality and suited for drying.

Cakes, cupcakes, sweets, and even teas and drinks would look lovely adorned with these freeze-dried cherry blossoms. These springtime sweets are as beautiful as they are delicious.

New Methods for Making Freeze-Dried Sweets

To help you take your freeze-dried candy-making to the next level, here are some tips:

Options for Flavoring and Seasoning

Play around with various flavorings and spices to give your freeze-dried sweets some diversity. Vanilla, almond, and mint extracts are all good options, as are spices like cinnamon, ginger, and cardamom. Flavored sugars or edible glitter are two more options for sprinkling on the glitz.

Tips for Presentation and Decoration

Add some flair to your freeze-dried sweets to make them more presentable. You may give your sweets a luxurious look by dipping them in melted chocolate or colored candy melts, drawing elaborate patterns on them using edible food markers or dusting them with edible shimmer or luster dust.

Mixing Freeze-Dried sweets

Freeze-dried sweets may be used to enhance the taste and texture of other desserts. Ice cream, yogurt, and pudding all taste great with a dusting of crushed freeze-dried fruits. You may also use them as an ingredient in other baked goods.

Creating Custom Freeze-Dried Candy Blends

Blend your own special freeze-dried candy by combining your favorite flavors of nuts, fruits, and sweets. This gives you the freedom to adjust the taste and texture to your liking. You may sprinkle these mixtures over foods, add them to trail mixes, or eat them on their own as snacks.

Some helpful hints for preserving the quality and freshness of your freeze-dried sweets during storage and packaging.

Keep them out of the reach of moisture by storing them in airtight containers or resealable bags. If you want to keep your food fresher for longer, you might use oxygen absorbers or moisture-absorbing sachets. Clearly identify which containers are which by labeling and dating them.

You may take your freeze-dried candy-making to the next level by experimenting with these sophisticated methods. Try new things and express your originality without reservation.

Conclusion

Finally, this freeze-dried candy guidebook provides a tasty variety of recipes and methods to spark your culinary imagination. Along the way, we learned about traditional freeze-dried sweets, chocolate-covered delicacies, fruit and nut bars, one-of-a-kind candy creations for festive occasions, and sophisticated methods for improving your candy-making abilities.

Candy bars that explode with a powerful taste and intriguing textures may be made by freeze-drying fruits, preserving their original colors, flavors, and nutritional content. This cookbook has everything you need to produce freeze-dried sweets that are both tasty and beautiful, whether you're an experienced candy maker or a passionate beginner.

Keep in mind that freeze-dried sweets are capable of bringing excitement and happiness to any event, whether it is a celebration or a simple moment of indulgence. Candies come in many forms and sizes, from the fun and quirky to the elegant and beautiful like those made from freeze-dried fruit or cherry blossoms.

Feel free to try new things and be creative while producing your own unique candies from freeze-dried ingredients. The only thing hindering you is your own inventiveness. Keep track of what works, modify it to your tastes, and then show it off to the people you care about.

It is my hope that the enchantment and sweetness contained within these pages will encourage you to try your hand at freeze-dried candy manufacturing. Get your ingredients together, turn on the freeze drier, and start cooking!

Have fun creating confectionery and freeze-drying food!

In affectionate consideration,

Sally

Made in United States
Troutdale, OR
01/06/2025

27545081R00046